R CUTE!

Owls

by Christina Leaf

BLASTOFF! READERS

BELLWETHER MEDIA · MINNEAPOLIS, MN

Note to Librarians, Teachers, and Parents:

Blastoff! Readers are carefully developed by literacy experts and combine standards-based content with developmentally appropriate text.

Level 1 provides the most support through repetition of high-frequency words, light text, predictable sentence patterns, and strong visual support.

Level 2 offers early readers a bit more challenge through varied simple sentences, increased text load, and less repetition of high-frequency words.

Level 3 advances early-fluent readers toward fluency through increased text and concept load, less reliance on visuals, longer sentences, and more literary language.

Level 4 builds reading stamina by providing more text per page, increased use of punctuation, greater variation in sentence patterns, and increasingly challenging vocabulary.

Level 5 encourages children to move from "learning to read" to "reading to learn" by providing even more text, varied writing styles, and less familiar topics.

Whichever book is right for your reader, Blastoff! Readers are the perfect books to build confidence and encourage a love of reading that will last a lifetime!

This edition first published in 2015 by Bellwether Media, Inc.

No part of this publication may be reproduced in whole or in part without written permission of the publisher. For information regarding permission, write to Bellwether Media, Inc., Attention: Permissions Department, 5357 Penn Avenue South, Minneapolis, MN 55419.

Library of Congress Cataloging-in-Publication Data

Leaf, Christina, author.
  Baby Owls / by Christina Leaf.
    pages cm. – (Blastoff! Readers. Super Cute!)
  Summary: "Developed by literacy experts for students in kindergarten through grade three, this book introduces baby owls to young readers through leveled text and related photos."– Provided by publisher.
  Audience: Ages 5-8.
  Audience: K to grade 3.
  Includes bibliographical references and index.
  ISBN 978-1-62617-172-5 (hardcover : alk. paper)
  1. Owls–Infancy–Juvenile literature. I. Title. II. Series: Blastoff! Readers. 1, Super Cute!
  QL696.S8L43 2015
  598.9'713192–dc23
                              2014035471

Table of Contents

Owlets!

Baby owls are
called owlets.
They **hatch**
from eggs.

Life in the Nest

Mom sits on the nest to keep it warm. Eggs hatch one at a time.

Newborn owlets are covered in fluffy **down**. These feathers keep them warm.

Dad brings
food to the nest.
Mom feeds it
to the owlets.

The babies **compete** for the food. They give loud **screeches** for attention.

Out and About

Soon the babies stretch their legs. They hop around the nest.

The owlets also flap their wings. They start with short flights.

Fledglings stay near the nest. They still need mom and dad for food.

Soon the owlets can find their own food. They fly from the nest for good. Up and away!

Glossary

compete–to fight

down–soft feathers that keep birds warm

fledglings–owlets that have just learned how to fly

hatch–to break out of an egg

newborn–just recently born

screeches–high-pitched cries

To Learn More

AT THE LIBRARY

Leaf, Christina. *Baby Ducks*. Minneapolis, Minn.: Bellwether Media, 2014.

Schuetz, Kari. *Owls*. Minneapolis, Minn.: Bellwether Media, 2012.

Waddell, Martin. *Owl Babies*. Cambridge, Mass.: Candlewick Press, 1992.

ON THE WEB

Learning more about owls is as easy as 1, 2, 3.

1. Go to www.factsurfer.com.

2. Enter "owls" into the search box.

3. Click the "Surf" button and you will see a list of related web sites.

With factsurfer.com, finding more information is just a click away.

Index